the Garfield Gallery 2

Jim Davis

RAVETTE BOOKS

First published by Ravette Books Limited 1992

Printed and bound for Ravette Books Limited
3 Glenside Estate, Star Road,
Partridge Green, Nr. Horsham,
West Sussex RH13 8RA
An Egmont Company
by STIGE, Italy

ISBN 1 85304 395 8

IF I DISGUISE MYSELF AS A BIRD, I SHOULD BE ABLE TO GET CLOSE ENOUGH FOR AN EASY LUNCH

GLUK
GLUK
GLUK

GLUE

SWIM FINS

WADDLE
WADDLE

JIM DAVIS

10-31   © 1982 United Feature Syndicate, Inc.

GOOD MORNING, GARFIELD. I'M SO HAPPY YOU CAN SHARE THIS GLORIOUS MORNING WITH ME

MICHELANGELO WOULD GIVE UP PAINTING IN A MINUTE IF HE SAW THE CANVAS MOTHER NATURE HAS RENDERED JUST FOR US TODAY

CHIRP CHIRP

JUST LISTEN TO THE SYMPHONY OF SOUND FROM NATURE'S FLUTE SECTION

AND THE PERFECT SIGHTS AND SOUNDS ARE PERFUMED WITH THESE LOVELY FLOWERS. WHAT DO YOU THINK, GARFIELD?

JIM DAVIS   12-19

YOU REALLY DON'T CARE, DO YOU?

BINGO

You know it's Monday when your down vest meets up with its former owner

JIM DAViS

WE CATS ARE VERY INDEPENDENT. WE DON'T NEED ANYBODY
ISN'T THAT RIGHT, POOKY?
JIM DAVIS

© 1981 United Feature Syndicate, Inc.

IF YOU CAN'T CONVINCE'M... CONFUSE'M

JIM DAVIS

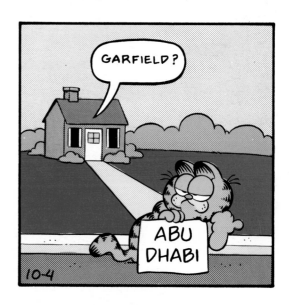

© 1981 United Feature Syndicate, Inc.

I KEEP MY AFFECTION
IN THE CLOSET

If I were to come back to earth, I'd like to come back as a pillow

JIM DAVIS

A DIET IS TOO LITTLE OF A GOOD THING

JIM DAVIS

Take this jog and shove it

JIM DAVIS

NEVER SHARPEN YOUR CLAWS ON A WATERBED

JIM DAVIS

Monday moves in a mysterious way

JiM DAViS

Diets are for people who want to belittle themselves

GARFIELD

JIM DAVIS

I LOVE TO
COURT DANGER

© 1983 United Feature Syndicate, Inc.

11-13

We must all learn to laugh at ourselves

Ever have a day when your timing was off?

JiM DAViS

WHEN IT COMES TO EATING, I'M A GENIUS

JIM DAVIS